William W. Handlin, Isaac T. Hinton

American Politics

A moral and political work, treating of the causes of the civil war, the

nature of government, and the necessity for reform

William W. Handlin, Isaac T. Hinton

American Politics
*A moral and political work, treating of the causes of the civil war, the nature of
government, and the necessity for reform*

ISBN/EAN: 9783337223991

Printed in Europe, USA, Canada, Australia, Japan

Cover: Foto ©Suzi / pixelio.de

More available books at **www.hansebooks.com**

AMERICAN POLITICS,

A MORAL AND POLITICAL WORK,

TREATING OF THE

Causes of the Civil War,

THE NATURE OF GOVERNMENT, AND THE NECESSITY FOR REFORM.

BY W. W. HANDLIN.

NEW ORLEANS:
PRINTED BY ISAAC T. HINTON, 27 COMMERCIAL PLACE.
1864.

CONTENTS.

PREFACE.

To those who are fond of fanciful and romantic writings, this short work will prove dry and uninteresting; while the more serious and practical may discover matter worthy of reflection, as well as pleasure, in meditating on many subjects of public and private interest. It is with great diffidence that I entrust myself on the sea of literature, and the doubts I entertain of my ability to please the public would deter me from any attempts at publication; but the hope of being of some service to my countrymen has induced me to make the experiment, and though the style adopted by me may often appear censorious, I freely confess that I deem it necessary to the object in view, as

> "The royal vices of our age demand
> A keener weapon and a mightier hand."

No doubt it is now apparent that there are some defects in our government which ought to be remedied, although it may be objected that it is impolitic to raise such questions, and many will contend that the Constitution is perfect; but if such is the case, it will stand the test of examination; and though nothing worthy of being adopted may be found here, others may discover improvements which will establish the government on a permanent basis and perpetuate the national existence.

- W W HANDLIN.

New Orleans, Oct. 25th, 1863.

2

AMERICAN POLITICS.

I. THE PRESIDENT.—The periodical election of the President of the United States, every four years, by the people, is, and has been, fraught with consequences of the utmost importance to the nation. For some time previous to that event, the masses of the people, either from their natural inclination, the influence of politicians, or the importance of the subject itself, are always stirred up by degrees, as it approaches, until the whole country is in a ferment. These commotions, (from which, in the heat of argument and faction, riots have often been created, and blood spilt,) continued to increase from one presidential election to another, until they finally culminated in civil war   Every one will admit that the true happiness of the people should ever be the aim and object of the government and it is questionable, to say the least, whether this continual changing of the Executive of the nation, which causes such a general disturbance of the body politic, is advantageous or injurious.   It is evident, also that the organization of the government of the United States, or the execution of its laws, is defective; for every well constituted government should be able to foresee dangers and prevent great public disasters before they take place, and it is certain that had it been perfect it would not now be reduced, by mere internal foes, to its present unhappy condition.

II. MONARCHICAL GOVERNMENTS.—From the earliest ages of the world mankind, in every country, have established for their government a supreme power for the order and well being of society   The most ancient form of government is the monarchical, which has been sustained in most countries to the present day, not only on account of its simplicity but for its certainty in establishing a fixed executive, whether the monarchy be absolute or limited.   Civil war is caused, usually, from disputes as to who shall be the true and acknowledged chief of the nation; and when that functionary is designated by some certain and infallible rule, the advantage to the true government, on the ground of legitimacy, in case its authority is disputed, is too clear to be questioned. But a monarchy, in this respect, is preferable to a republic, such as the present United States, because the executive, (that is, the king in the former and the president in the latter,) is more fixed, the terms of longer duration and the order of succession more natural and easy By that form of government, party dissensions and sectional prejudices are, in a great measure, eluded, and the true patriot looks, as it were, to the king as the person ordained by fate to govern the nation, and considers it his duty to love and honor him, whether he be able or imbecile, through his country, and to serve it through him. . If, however, some republican form of government could be devised, which would secure to the people the election of members of Congress, and at the same time provide against the evils of party, general and frequent elections of the President, as well as those arising occasionally from the imbecility of hereditary sovereigns, it would approach somewhat nearer to perfection.

III. UNIVERSAL SUFFRAGE.—As the government of the United States is based upon a purely democratic form, it follows that every freeman at the age of majority is entitled to all the rights, privileges and immunities of an American citizen. How far this universal right of interfering with, or controlling the most important affairs of the country should be extended to some who have no qualifications, except that of age, to entitle them to such high privileges, is a matter of grave consideration. For many years past, the elections, in most of our large cities at least, have been entirely under the influence of the most worthless part of the community, who have controlled, in a great measure, all public affairs, while men of substance and respectability, whose vital interests were at stake, have been either disgusted, or deterred from going to the polls. The men, in many localities, who have most influence in elections, have not only been without any visible means of support, but mere stragglers, and frequenters of bar rooms, making it a business to secure emolument and advancement by their professional assistance, so that few men of real worth cared to obtain office under such auspices, and consequently the country was left to its fate. The right of suffrage should be a sacred thing, and it should contribute towards true and just government, and not be converted into an engine to raise up the crafty, and those who have the least interest in society

IV   It is difficult to conceive why a man who has no family, property or profession, and who has never done any thing for himself or his country, should be allowed to vote, and not only control the interests of the country at large, but also those of honest and industrious citizens. An excess in Democracy is, without doubt, as injurious as an excess in any thing else, and to curtail within proper limits the inestimable privilege of free suffrage would be a service to the Republic. By fixing certain qualifications, which would require some position and standing of the voter, it would be in some degree an honor to enjoy that privilege; and, hence, young men would have a certain goal before them, which would stimulate their ambition and make them desirous of attaining it. But why should those who have no fixed establishment or domicil, no property upon which to pay taxes, nor any intellectual qualification, which should form an exception, desire to direct or control public affairs? They should be content to wait until they should acquire those qualifications which would not only give them knowledge and experience, but make them feel an interest in the exercise of the right of suffrage. It very often happens that those who are without means or occupation, and consequently have no interest at stake, are the most busy in attending to the affairs of others, which, as a general thing, gives rise to mischief. If, therefore, none were allowed to vote but tax-payers, or persons having a homestead, however humble, and certain literary and other men, distinguished by their art or usefulness, more benefit would be derived from the elective franchise.

V DEMAGOGUES.—It is generally admitted on all sides that the present civil war, with all its attendant evils, has been the work of demagogues, and that really the great masses of the people had but little to do with it until dragged into the vortex by necessity These men, who were originally without useful occupations, or who had been unfortunate in business, were never more happy than when raising some new political question by which to flatter and cajole the populace.

and thereby gain for themselves honors, rewards
and reputation. With liberty, the rights of the
people, and democracy in their mouths, they succeeded in making almost every American citizen
believe that he was not only an absolute and
independent potentate himself, but that neither
love nor respect was due either to the government, or its highest and most worthy officials.
Laws were not respected, and the Constitution
was the victim which those disturbers of the
public peace continually mutilated and sacrificed, in order to supply themselves with matter
for the purpose of fostering and perpetuating
unnecessary agitation. The jealousy of the people has been so aroused concerning their rights,
that all offices, in most of the States, are filled
by election, and their terms are so short that even
the incompetent incumbents have no time to
learn, and are chiefly employed in endeavors to
obtain or secure their places.

VI. Mr Volney, in his Ruins of Palmyra,
endeavors, as it would seem, to overturn and destroy all religions hitherto existing amongst mankind, without inventing or substituting any thing
else in their place, notwithstanding the universal

3

tendency of human nature to have some kind of worship. It is doubtless, therefore, the duty of every one who finds fault to propose some remedy, so as not to leave matters in a worse condition than they were before. Now, if the people at large would be more careful in choosing their public officers and representatives, and see that none but substantial men, whose interests were identified with their own, were chosen, instead of noisy striplings, without knowledge or experience, it is evident that the dignity and welfare of the country would be better supported. But, throughout the land, politics have been abandoned to the young and idle, as matters of light or trifling concern, while old and respectable men, either from diffidence, or a desire of ease, have remained in retirement and without influence, when not only their own, but the most vital interests of the Republic were at stake. The terms of office should be longer, judges should be appointed, electioneering and demagogism should be discountenanced, and a more deep concern should be felt in public affairs, without the noise and strife which have gradually increased until they have demoralized and corrupted the more conservative principles of the days of Washington.

VII. LIBERTY OF THE PRESS.—There can be
no doubt that a certain independent tone and
freedom of expression ought to be allowed to
public journals; and those whose business it is to
watch passing events and make true reports and
just comments on them, ought to maintain a
true, manly spirit, and not be obliged to concili-
ate jealous and tyrannical governors. In the
United States, however, the newspapers have so
increased in power and numbers as almost to
sway the destinies of the nation. Paper, and the
free schools, have produced many oracles of the
quill, and "every mountain now hath found a
tongue." Not that public schools are objection-
ble, for they are good in their place, but because
something more than a common education is
necessary for the discussion of matters of state.
There may be, and no doubt are, many learned
and able editors whose instructions are of great
benefit to the people, but it cannot be denied that
there are thousands of scribblers without either
learning or experience, who attempt to discourse
in their *leaders* on international law, and grave
questions of foreign policy, when they have
scarcely ever been beyond the limits of their
own towns, and have about as much knowledge

of the world, and the science of government, as school boys. Without ever having looked into a book on public or municipal law, they write in the most careless, presumptuous and reckless manner. These men, too, arrogate to themselves the right of passing judgment indiscriminately on men and things, and have so little respect for authority, or the dignity of office, that they seldom fail to seize upon any occasion to ridicule the government and bring it into contempt, and thus largely infuse the same spirit into the masses, simply to advance party interests. They should be taught that liberty is not license, and that a proper decorum should be observed in treating the affairs of a great nation.

VIII. But what greater or more objectionable censorship can there be over the press than that established by politicians and party leaders? Few journalists dare to produce any thing in their columns which may appear distasteful to certain magnates of their party, or which may endanger their own popularity with those on whose patronage they depend. In this way, then, the people seldom find facts and questions of public or political importance represented in

their true colors, and plain truth is so perverted
or mystified that one is often more confused than
enlightened by reading a newspaper. Not only
this; but politicians of the character in question
have become so astute that they assume the traits
common to diplomatists of foreign courts, and
continually feel the public pulse, and balance
themselves between the populace and political
leaders, so as to advance their peculiar party
interests, regardless of the general good. So it
is, therefore, that under the present system of
public papers, men read not so much what is useful and true, as that which tends to promote the
views of designing politicians, and in this way
sectional prejudices are deepened and perpetuated, national sentiment is suppressed or extin-
guished, and all the fiery and angry passions of
men are aroused, agitated and embittered, while
peace, innocence and tranquility, so necessary to
the happiness of a people, incontinently take
their flight, and the country is plunged into all
the horrors of civil war. If, therefore, the
national character of this kind of writing is not
improved, it behooves every one to be on his
guard, and estimate it at its proper value, so as
not to allow his partizan and local prejudices to
take entire possession of him.

IX. FREE SPEECH.—It is one of the grandest
privileges of republican institutions, that every
individual is allowed to express his opinions
freely on all subjects, and, indeed, it is this great
principle which has contributed so much towards
relieving the human soul from its thraldom, and
at the same time developed the vast resources and
latent energies of the untrammeled mind. How
beautiful it is, for example, to see honest and
industrious farmers or mechanics discuss, in
their leisure moments, questions of public policy
or general utility, which may be of doubtful
expediency, and in this manner arrive at just
and sound conclusions. At the same time, they
feel that they are protected, that they are interested, and that they possess that quiet, manly
and undisturbed freedom which gives rise to
every noble and generous action. While, however, this right of free speech is so dear to the
American people, and is enjoyed by them in
such an eminent degree, it should not be abused,
and if one born on American soil should so far
forget himself, and be so lost to all noble and patriotic sentiments as to traduce his own country
and government, and desire to see foreign alliances formed, or a foreign sceptre introduced.

(as has often happened in the South of late,)
such a man should not only be deprived of
free speech, but he should be punished as being
guilty of one of the most degrading and dangerous crimes. If, therefore, it is considered to what
dangerous results seditious language may give
rise—riots, treason and revolution—it is certainly
the policy of every well ordered government to
suppress it, and not allow liberal discussion to be
so far abused as to endanger the public safety

X. RESPECT.—When society and government
are formed from the rude elements of the human
character in its natural state, there is a tacit or
express agreement that certain individuals, des-
tined either by nature, circumstance or choice,
shall direct and control all matters of public
import. This is necessary, for otherwise, there
could be no organization, and the weak would be
at the mercy of the strong, while progress and
civilization would be impossible. How important it is, then, that those who are called to rule
should be assisted and respected by the common-
alty in furtherance of the general welfare. But
among Americans this spirit has become well
nigh extinct, and ultra democracy has inspired

them with contempt for all constituted authority. With the idea that governors are servants, and that the governed are immaculate, the character of public men has lost cast, and our lawfully constituted authorities lack dignity as well in the eyes of foreign nations as in our own moreover, there is a constant desire of change and innovation. Nor is it less important that superiors should be sustained and respected, when we consider the efficacy of law; for if the men who make and execute the laws want dignity or respect, a corresponding decrease will be found in the respect and obedience to those laws. We should, consequently, be satisfied as American citizens, that we actually enjoy more freedom than men in other parts of the world, without detracting from those whose good fortune has placed them above us, since their authority, though it weigh upon us a little, is indispensable to government. Great caution should be observed in passing judgment on public officers, or imputing to them improper motives without good grounds: "Suspicions amongst thoughts are like bats amongst birds—they ever fly by twilight." There is nothing more common than the censure of those in authority, and many believe with facility that public officers are corrupt, and should be removed, when really, in most cases, there is no foundation in fact, and when it is considered that those who serve the public have no freedom, and are often the most unhappy of men, while discharging their laborious duties, they are not to be envied, but are entitled to much charity and indulgence

XI. PROTECTION.—The generality of mankind desire peace and tranquility, so that they can pursue their respective avocations unmolested. and know and feel that they can count with certainty upon the safety and prosperity of all their social occupations and enterprizes. It is the duty of the government to afford that security, and in fact, it is its principal object to bring about that result. There are always comparatively few in every country who delight in the agitation of politics, and who make it their business to stir up the people on abstract or chimerical questions, which will eventually result in their own elevation, and these few are usually of that class who do not belong to the most substantial part of the community, but engage in such pursuits for want of better occupation. and press

4

then selves forward rather by their own assurance than by their merit. They are supported by the populace more on account of the noise they make than for any proofs of talent or devotion to their country It follows, then, that the less there is done in the government by such people the better, and the more simple the government is, the more the danger of disturbance will be diminished. It is certainly undesirable that the whole people should be all the time engaged in carrying on the government, and it is this very thing which is complained of by those who live in countries harrassed by perpetual wars, they say they cannot live in quietude, and that they are compelled to take part in public disturbances against their will. The excellency of a good government is to afford protection to its people, so that they may enjoy that true freedom of pursuing their private occupations according to their own inclinations, with the gratifying consciousness that there is a superior power which provides for their safety and happiness.

XII. THE ACTUAL CONDITION.—But how is it with our governments, local and general, in the United States? The complicated nature of

public offices, the short terms of their tenure, the
frequent elections, and the usual means employed
to secure popular favor, make what should be
esteemed the most honorable positions. mere
objects of mercenary intrigues, and the masses
are used by the cunning to carry out the work
which is already laid down and marked out.
Thus it happens that there is constantly some
excitement concerning changes which are to be
made in office, when comparatively few are interested, and false issues are paraded to increase
party spirit. The government gets into the
hands of bad men, and when, in the height of
some election excitement, civil war breaks out,
there is no power to stop it, and good citizens
with the rest are left at the mercy of the lawless.
Who does not know that heretofore, in perhaps
every State, the principles, nominees, platforms
and plans of every party have been under the control of half a dozen men, who have formed their
cliques, and held their caucuses in some obscure
club room? It is well known, too, how the willing crowd have ranged themselves under the
banners thus hoisted before them, and blindly
followed their leaders. when really there was no
cause for excitement: or, if there was. they did

not understand it. This is the fault of too much republicanism, which makes the people at large subject to demagogues, and abuses the elective system. It may work well in the beginning, when the government is young and men are more virtuous, but, when the windy storms and tempests of more degenerate days shall come, the fabric will fall from its own agitation. Eternal vigilance is the price of liberty, but eternal commotion will cause dissolution.

XIII. THE REMEDY.—A more conservative policy should be adopted. Every good citizen should never fail to vote, instead of staying at home, as heretofore, and allowing elections to be controlled by low politicians, drunkards and thugs. Elections should be dispensed with as far as consistent with democratic government. Good men for governors should be elected, and they should be allowed to appoint judges, so that the judiciary would not be dependent on party favor. It is every citizen's duty to go to the polls and cast his vote where not only the good of the state, and the welfare of his neighbor are concerned, but his own eventual peace and prosperity depend upon the performance of all his civil functions. And yet

how many of the best men in the country entirely
neglect the affairs of the public, and act with as
much indifference as if they were foreign subjects.
But it is particularly the duty of old men, whose
wisdom is fortified by experience, and men of
wealth and leisure, who are less venal than others,
to look after the interests of the public, instead of
which, they usually retire and throw themselves
into the lap of luxury, forgetful of their country's
claims, or considering that such employment is
unworthy of them; whereas, nothing is more noble
than the service of the state. Then the influence of cliques would be weakened, and politics
would assume a more respectable standard. The
people would really govern then; and their government would be raised from that low condition
which familiarity inspires, to one of dignity and
strength. It was said by one, that "knowledge is
power;" but then, dignity would be power, and
justice would follow in the footsteps of decorum.

XIV —Mexico.—It is almost universally true,
that the mere imitator, without natural and individual qualifications, will never succeed. Mexico endeavored to imitate the United States, not
only in forming a republic, but in basing it upon

a number of States, as the United States had
done. But the States were made for that purpose, out of what had been formerly one government, to-wit. the vice royalty of New Spain;
while in the United States the government was
formed out of pre-existing separate States, which
were, after much deliberation, united into one
nation. From the fact that there is a great pre-
ponderance of Indian blood in Mexico and the
common people are uneducated, it may well be
doubted whether they are suited to the republican form of government, but when that republic
becomes more complicated than ours, by forming
new States where none existed, with all the par-
aphernalia of State legislation and governors, the
project proves itself to be impracticable. Each
one of those governors and representatives of the
people soon becomes a chieftain, and being ambitious of power, raises an army and promulgates
a *pronunciamiento*. The people are poor and
ignorant, and being of an idle and roving disposition, they are easily led to espouse any cause
which opposes the party in power and affords
them an opportunity for support and plunder.
They need a strong government of some kind,
and perhaps a republic, in a more simple form,
would suit them as well as any other.

XV   But the United States has pursued a most miserable policy towards her sister, Mexico. Almost from the beginning she has acted the part of a cold and selfish individual, whose conduct is often interspersed with an outward show of friendship and sympathy; while she has steadily sought her own aggrandizement at the expense of her magnanimity   When the revolution in Texas occurred, the United States was secretly at the bottom of it, and her grasping and ungenerous conduct caused the war which resulted in dispossessing Mexico of half her domain. It is doubtful whether this vast accession of territory will prove of ultimate advantage to the United States, and especially the part of it lying on the Pacific may give the government trouble at some future day   But after the forces of the United States had occupied the capital of Mexico, and secured to her such immense concessions, instead of taking her by the arm and placing her on a firm footing, she silently withdrew, leaving her weak neighbor a prey to a thousand dangers.   Nor is the United States to be pitied now that a foreign Prince, in the hour of trial, steps in and proposes to furnish Mexico with a permanent government.   The United

States long had it in her power to have done better for her natural ally, but failed, perhaps more from a hope of absorbing her territory, should her future incapacity produce such an effect, than from any fear of "entangling alliances." These are some of the wrongs done by the United States to Mexico, and it may be that the former is now suffering the penalty which always follows injustice.

XVI. How noble it would have been for the United States, after the war with Mexico, to have taken her under her protection, and assisted her in maintaining peace and good government with a disinterested and magnanimous spirit! Mexico, who had held up the United States as a model, and beacon light to guide her in the experiment of republicanism, would have leaned upon her friendly arm until her own increasing strength could have supported her What bloody scenes would have been prevented! How many of the noble sons of Mexico, who have been cruelly sacrificed in their unmeaning, fratricidal wars, would still live to serve mankind!

But aside from all considerations of humanity, it would have been the true policy of the United

States, at the close of the Mexican war, or since, to have assisted Mexico in establishing peace and good government. It is well known what immense exports of valuable productions were once shipped from that country; and from its contiguous position to the United States, on the Gulf of Mexico, its trade to Americans would have been of incalculable advantage. The prosperity of the Mexicans is the prosperity of the Americans, for just so much as the area of the commerce of the one is increased, just so much also is the field of operations of the other enlarged. It is, then, a blind, a selfish policy, to allow the prosperity of Mexico to be retarded by foolish and interminable civil wars. And as there can be no doubt that the territory of the United States is sufficiently extensive, and that it would be impolitic to increase it by accessions from Mexico, the real desire should be to see the latter increase in wealth and commercial importance, so that traffic with her would be advantageous. War has created some antipathy between the two races, and the haughty American is inclined to look with contempt on his less prosperous neighbor; but it would be advantageous for Americans to adopt some of the social habits and character-
5

ıstics of that well mannered and gentle race, in whom evident traces of the noble hidalgo still linger.

XVII. SLAVERY.—It has been said by some, that slavery had nothing to do with the war, but the simple fact that one of the belligerents maintained slavery, while the other was free, is sufficient to contradict and disprove the assertion. Upon that institution the prejudices of both sections of the country have been built up and perpetuated. Still, it never would have disturbed the peace of the country had it not been for the constant agitation caused by electioneering poli· ticians and the baleful influence of ultra democracy and popular sovereignty Slavery was the constant theme both North and South, upon which candidates for office loved to dwell, and the people of both sections were equally misrepresented, the one to the other, until such a mutual hatred was inspired, that both were ready for war on the first signal. This hatred was carefully instilled into the people by politicians and newspapers, and such care was taken of their education in this respect, that very little of the truth was ever proclaimed by the orator, or ever

appeared in the public prints. In the South,
the Abolitionists were represented as cut-throats
and robbers, and in fact nothing was so mean,
but they were still more so. In the North, the
Southern planters were held up as barbarians,
and compared unfavorably with the cannibals of
Africa. But where was the necessity for all this
disturbance? One should be willing to allow
his neighbor to live in peace. If slavery was an
evil, the Southern States were responsible for it;
and they certainly were competent to manage
their local concerns. The Southern States might
in time have got rid of the institution, or at least
corrected its abuses.

XVIII. Examining the question in a purely
moral point of view, slavery in the United States
has undoubtedly ameliorated the condition of the
African, and when it is considered that negroes
were introduced into this country without any
complicity of the present owners of slaves, whose
fortunes mainly consist in this species of property, it would certainly be most unjust to make
them bear the whole burden of advancing the
public good, and free their slaves without compen-
sation. But the slaves in the South, to a great

extent, are as happy as the generality of mankind. They are, the same as others, creatures of habit, and being in a subordinate condition, they never feel oppressed by restrictions, but on the contrary, are more fitted for that state than any other. They have been brought from a barbarous country, where they were not only savage and useless, but a disgrace to the human race. In their present condition they greatly increase the wealth and industry of the world, while their intercourse with a more advanced race has communicated to them greater intelligence, and they at the same time have the benefits of the Christian religion. But granting that their condition is hard, how foolish it is to endeavor to raise mankind above trouble and sorrow! Look at the thousands of cases in the North and in England where misery and degradation can never be relieved! All are slaves more or less, and besides, the laws of nature and of health, together with our passions and prejudices, exact of us the most rigorous discipline. However desirable it may be to form a perfect government, where all shall be happy, still every wise law-giver will doubtless consider the subject utopian.

XIX. ABUSES.—Nevertheless, it cannot be denied that the institution of slavery exists in an aggravated form in the South, and could some of its harshest features be obliterated it might unquestionably be considered a blessing to the African race. There can be nothing more revolting to human nature than the constant practice of separating husbands from their wives and mothers from their children, and if this custom looks objectionable to Southerners themselves, how must it appear to persons educated in countries where slavery does not exist? But the people of the South have been so embittered by the resistance of the North to the execution of the fugitive slave law, and the intermeddling spirit of the Abolitionists, that they have made the burden of slavery more intolerable than ever before, from the time of the Roman Empire to the present day In Rome, the emancipation of the slave was favored by the laws, but of late in some parts of the South, the slave cannot be emancipated, and it is forbidden by statute that he shall be instructed, or permitted to hire his own time. The contrary course should be pursued. The slave market should be abolished, and it should no longer be permitted to degrade our large cities with slave pens, where human beings are exhibited for sale, in rows like cattle in market stalls. For the sake of morality and all the finer feelings of the soul, men should not be torn from their wives and mothers separated from their children.

XX. AMELIORATION.—On large plantations it would be easy to establish a custom, which often happens now, of selling the slaves with the soil, so that they become, as it were, fixtures, and live with their families, enjoying the privilege of cultivating small lots of ground for themselves. The small property allowed to slaves by the Roman law was called the *peculium*, and many American planters grant their slaves the privilege of possessing it. But, it is said, such a policy would lessen the value of slaves. Suppose it would, it would then cause their owners to get rid of them, or find some other species of labor, and then an acknowledged evil would be remedied, or at least mitigated. But why should the whites be so selfish as to want all the benefits, without allowing the common rights of humanity to the blacks? In such a condition, the negroes would be infinitely more happy than if left entirely to themselves, as they naturally require some direction, at least so far as their capacity is at present developed, in order to be useful to themselves and others. Then they could be instructed in morality and christianity, and be gradually prepared, as fast as occasion occurred, to return to their original homes, and be instrumental in redeeming a vast continent from the thraldom of intellectual night. Why the South has not pursued some such course, for the sake of humanity and civilization, can only be accounted for from considerations of self-interest and the inordinate thirst for gain, which is nowhere more deeply implanted than among Americans.

XXI. THE GREAT DIFFICULTY—But the most important question is, what is to be done with the negroes after they are liberated? It is obvious to every one that if they were left entirely to themselves, in their present uneducated and unprepared state, without lands or habitations, they would become a public charge, and bring ruin and decay upon a great portion of the country Why, then, should philanthropists advocate the unqualified abolition of slavery, without pointing out the means of avoiding this great difficulty? It is clear that the present generation of slaves, at

least, would suffer infinitely more, if suddenly
made free, than they do in their present condition, and the dangers to the whites, above all
those to which the state would be subjected, from
the unnatural equalization and amalgamation
of races, would produce ruin and degradation.
Mountains are not removed in a day, and therefore it is necessary to be guided by reason, and
pursue such a moderate and well digested method
as will eradicate the evil of slavery without bringing ruin and destruction upon the country, causing, at the same time, irreparable injury to both
masters and servants. In the event that the
negroes were all turned loose upon the country,
and allowed to stroll from place to place, at will,
it would become necessary for the State legisla-
tures to pass such rigid laws and police regulations, punishing vagrants and compelling idle
persons to remain at home and work, or be compelled to labor on public works, that although
the name might be changed, negroes would still
be slaves. As long as the blacks remain in the
United States, in connection with the whites,
there will be trouble, and all the fine theories of
humanitarians will not be able to remove this
difficulty

XXII. ARISTOCRACY.—The tendency of the institution of slavery is to establish a powerful aristocracy, and in fact, this class has been so influential in the South as to control and direct all non-slaveholders and bind them to their policy. To this influence may be ascribed the direct cause of the war. Slavery produces a disposition to rule without impediment, and hence, powerful men, who have been accustomed to be obeyed from their infancy, by hundreds of slaves, cannot brook opposition in matters of government, and consider themselves greatly superior to ordinary men. Consequently, they become haughty, secluded, and think more of their own importance than their duties towards mankind. At the same time, this state of society produces a corresponding sense of humiliation and want of self-respect among the poor, and they become careless of their own, as well as the public prosperity, so that a certain lethargy and want of enterprise are observable in all slave countries. But slave aristocracy, above all others, is more anti-social, for the natural disposition to compare, causes slave owners to look upon poor people as only being equal to, or at least but little above, the slaves by whom they are surrounded; so that they can only

6

associate with other slave owners, or persons whom, by some accident, they consider equal to themselves. Men of this character are apt to consider that they form a species of nobility, and that if they have not had titles conferred upon them by the sovereign, so as to distinguish them from the common people, it is no fault of theirs. Whereas, in truth, all their importance is derived from no noble deed, but rests upon the abject service of degraded human beings.

XXIII. AGAINST NATIONAL POLICY.—There is something which is often not expressed in constitutions or laws, called national policy, and which may be described as that which is most useful or advantageous to the nation. Now, the institution of slavery is certainly contrary to the national policy of the United States, since it has caused war and come near destroying the integrity of the government itself. But it is the interest of the government to establish a similarity of thought, manners, customs and institutions. as far as possible, throughout the country. so as to give a national character to the people. This can never be done while there exists such an anti-republican element in one portion of the country as

African slavery On the contrary, the longer
this custom is continued the more will the different sections become estranged from each other,
and the more inimical will their interests be. In
republics, however, it is more essential than in
all other governments that homogenious institutions should prevail, as the people themselves are
to govern; and it is impossible for them to live
harmoniously when the most discordant elements
are fostered and perpetuated. When there is no
law, or when a foreign law is invoked, the judge
will disregard the prayer, if it is plainly in opposition to the interests of the country, or *contra
bonos mores.* If, on the other hand, there is a
law, however iniquitous it may be, he has no
choice, but must pass sentence in accordance
therewith. But in this latter case it is clear that
the State should take the matter in hand and
change the law in a proper manner, so that justice might be done thereafter. Now, if slavery
is protected by the Constitution, and yet is contrary to the policy of the nation, it becomes
necessary to change that Constitution and get
rid of the institution in accordance with the
principles of justice, and at the most practicable
period.

XXIV GRADUAL EMANCIPATION.—There can be no way of freeing the nation of this evil, so natural, so easy and so beneficial to all concerned, as that of gradual emancipation. Men do not feel the imaginary losses of their children, or those of future generations, so keenly as they do their own present losses, and will, therefore, more readily consent to lose a portion of this species of property gradually at some time in the future, and the next generation may be deprived of it altogether. Besides, it will not so interfere with their projects of fortune, and their usefulness as good citizens will not be destroyed. By this method the government may devise means to remove freed men, from time to time, to some more genial clime, where they will be of no further annoyance to the white race, and where they may enjoy the blessing of liberty without the consciousness of any superior race. It might also be practicable to give these people some isolated tract of country within the territory of the United States, as has been done with the Indians, where they would be directly under the protection of the government, and at the same time contribute to its wealth and power; provided, however, that they could be kept, to some extent, separate and distinct from the whites. This policy would be of much greater benefit to the negroes than the sudden abolition of slavery, for then they would be gradually prepared and educated for a different state of life, and their removal from the country would be carried on so imperceptibly that neither commerce nor agriculture would materially suffer by the change, while those that went before would prepare for those that came afterwards. On this view of the subject, it is apparent that all Americans, who have the good of the country at heart, should lay down their local prejudices and unite as one man in purging the country of this or any other evil, so as to maintain forever the grandeur, power and glory of this free American nation, which was founded by great and good men, and transmitted to their descendants as a never fading inheritance under the kind protection of Divine Providence.

XXV CAUSES OF THE CIVIL WAR.—The institution of slavery has, doubtless, been the true cause of secession and rebellion, although there have been many who have disputed the proposition, and alleged that the tariff and other questions were more powerful agents in causing

the South to throw off her allegiance and seek
protection from the injustice of the North in a
separate and independent government. Even
the agents of the Confederacy in Europe were
reported to have declared that slavery had nothing to do with the division of the country, and
that other and different subjects of grief were
relied on to justify the action of the South.
Indeed, it was said they represented to foreign
powers at one time, that the Confederacy itself
was not averse to liberating the slaves, provided
it could obtain the recognition and support of
their governments. But it is readily perceived
by any one conversant with the history of the
times, that the Southern people had no intention
of abandoning the titles to their slaves, and that
if such professions were made, the object was
simply to enable them to establish their sovereignty with the aid of foreign nations first, and
then trust to their ability to secure their slave
property afterwards. On the basis, therefore,
that slavery was the true and only cause of the
civil war, without which it never would have
occurred, it is interesting to observe the various
phases of the quarrel, the long and smothered
resentment of partisan leaders, the political cap-

ital afforded by the question, and the intense
sectional hatreds which were studiously educated into the people both North and South, until
the excess of passion and public excitement culminated in open revolt and uncompromising
secession. It may well be exclaimed, what a
curse slavery has been to Americans, and how
nearly they begin to resemble, in their propen-
sity to destroy each other, the aboriginal people
whom they have well nigh swept from the face
of the continent!

XXVI. THE MISSOURI COMPROMISE.—The
agitation of the slavery question caused serious
apprehension amongst American statesmen from
the earliest period of the history of the government, and that apprehension became still more
alarming as the subject began to assume a prominent political character. From the speculations
of philanthropists, and the publications of abolitionists, the question began to be discussed in
some anti-slavery districts by candidates for
office, and was afterwards introduced into the
United States Congress in, the form of ablition
petitions, which were laid on the table. The
struggle between the North and the South as to

whether the new Territories should be converted into free or slave States, next attracted the attention of the world, and then it was, that the true epoch and real contest for extension or extinction began. It was finally settled that all territory north of 36′ 30″, north latitude, should be, and remain, forever free, and this compact was denominated "the Missouri Compromise." This, though feeble, was one step towards liberty, still, it was a question of power, and Congress was willing to give to each section an equal share of the new Territories, that they might afterwards be better able to contend with each other: but the North, owing to the superiority of free institutions, far outstripped the South, and became much more populous and powerful. If the American representatives had decreed, on that occasion, that no new territory should ever become a slave State, it would doubtless have been better for the country, as it would have fixed a policy upon the national government and weakened the institution, so as to have left it powerless for evil.

XXVII. Not content with this great triumph, the Southern politicians were careful to lose none

of the numerous opportunities, which were constantly afforded them by the abolitionists, of
pushing their advantage, and extending their
conquests in the cause of human bondage. A
powerful logician, and a strict advocate for legal
rights, Stephen A. Douglas, demonstrated to the
American Congress that the line of 36' 30" was
unconstitutional, and that it should never have
been drawn so as to restrict slavery to the territory south of that line, and thus the foundation
upon which a dangerous subject had quietly slept
was torn up, and the march of slavery towards
the hesperian regions seemed to be favored by the
nation's counsellors. But why should that line
have been disturbed, whether it was constitu-
tional or not? Was it the true *policy* of the
nation to extend slavery towards the north or
west? Clearly, it was not. Being an evil, as
is generally admitted, it should not have been
extended. The institution is injurious to the
prosperity of the country, as is proved by a com-
parison between the free and the slave States,
since the former are much more prosperous,
therefore, the government should have taken a
decided course, regardless of the rigid constitu-
tional right, if there was such a right, to convey

7

slaves, as property, into the Territories. It is said, with some truth, that the Constitution should have been changed first; but where was the use, if such a policy was right? The government is not to act exactly like a judge who decides between party and party. but it is to act for the general good of the nation, without too nice legal distinctions. The law cannot be applied in all its strictness to the government as to individuals, for example, the sovereign cannot be sued. England has no formal Constitution. and still she is well governed by a national policy. based on certain great ͺrinciples, not but that a Constitution is, however, the best foundation for a government, while its tenets should not be so construed as to contravene the real interests of the nation and subvert its true policy

XXVIII. KANSAS.—Next came the memorable agitation of the question in Congress, as to whether slave owners should be allowed to settle in the common territory, called Kansas, most of which lay north of the line of 36' 30", and carry with them their slave property under the protection of the Constitution and laws of the United States. Here, Mr Douglas seemed to oppose the establishment of slavery in that Territory, although he had proved a powerful champion for slavery in the question of the Missouri Compromise line, on the ground that the institution was not suited to that Territory, and that the *people* would always decide for themselves whether it was beneficial or not; but it was evident that there must be a majority of anti-slavery men in Kansas from the large northern immigration. He was unquestionably a man of a good heart, and his errors are entitled to some extenuation, when it is considered that he argued more like a lawyer than a statesman, and that he was prompted by a laudable ambition, and aspired to the highest honors of the nation. At that time there was no question so prominent in politics as that of slavery, and none so well calculated to bring a public man into notoriety But how weak and unwise it was in the Congress of the United States to allow a few thousand adventurers, many of whom were, doubtless, fugitives from justice,· who had *squatted* almost beyond the pale of civilization, to throw the whole country into commotion, and endanger the peace and liberty of the people on account of mere abstract theories, when there was no real advantage to be gained, and the whole population of Kansas was hardly worth its attention.

XXIX. However, passion needs no foundation, and when a nation is governed by excitement and party feeling, no wise or politic measure can be expected. The South had been successful in carrying most of its political schemes, and, consequently, the Southern people were still more determined to carry their point at this period, and make Kansas a slave State, although it was clearly contrary to the national policy, and the country itself was totally unfitted for slave labor. Societies were formed in South Carolina and other States of the South for the purpose of aiding emigrants favorable to slavery to settle in Kansas, so as to secure a pro-slavery majority when the Territory should be converted into a State; while, on the other hand, Montgomery and others, assisted by the abolitionists in the North, who supplied them with Sharpe's rifles, were equally as active in their opposition to the project. Kansas then became the field on which the civil war, in miniature, first began, and instead of suppressing it in the outset, the generous politicians and statesmen, into whose

hands the government had fallen, were willing
to see fair play, and allow the two sections,
already stirred up to the highest pitch of frenzy,
to test their strength and powers on this neutral
ground. The President, too, seemed equally
undecided, if, indeed, he was not a supporter of
the South in this matter, belonging, as he did, to
the Democratic party, which was the strongest in
that section. And it is difficult to conceive how
the party advocating slavery in Kansas could
have succeeded so far, had it not been favored
by the administration. At any rate, it is certain
that that President did nothing to prevent the
civil war which afterwards broke out, and which
might have been easily checked by vigilant
measures. But as that war was chiefly brought
on by the Democratic party to which he belonged,
and which had been defeated by the election, it
is possible that he was not seriously opposed to
it. On the other hand, many good men voted
the Democratic ticket from mere *routine* and
habit, not dreaming that the defeat of Mr. Breck-
enridge would cause a war, but supposing that
the excitement would pass away as in other
presidential elections. How could the country
escape danger when it was controlled by con-

tending factions, which were willing to sacrifice
its best interests, in order to gratify their own
private animosities?

XXX. SECTIONAL PREJUDICES.—By this time
the people of the two sections had become so
embittered against each other, that they lost
sight of all national pride, and began to consider
that there was nothing in common between them;
that they were different in races, and that, above
all, the "inevitable negro," whether for slavery
or freedom, was the paramount object of consideration. Whether this state of anti-national feeling proceeded from the people, or whether it was
entirely kindled and nourished by party leaders
and public men of one kind or another, is of
little importance, as the effect would always be
the same. But it is certain that politicians, both
North and South, generally speaking, as well as
newspaper editors, instead of trying to calm the
fury of the people, did all they could to fan it
into a flame. And last, not least, clergymen
of different denominations, whose duty it was to
take care of the spiritual welfare of mankind,
used the sanctity of their calling in creating dissensions in the national family, and perpetuating

sectional rancor, which must one day satiate itself with blood. Instead of this suicidal course, it is strange that such a national policy could not have been adopted as would have welded the two sections together in one common destiny If, however, that was impossible, it is clear that the government should have been prepared long before, to assert and maintain its power, and at the same time overawe traitors, who would tear down the temple of liberty under the guise of Secession and States Rights. Any other kind of government is not worth the name.

Since the war has commenced, more especially, slavery prejudices have been more fully developed. Wherever the Federal armies have gone, the institution has been virtually destroyed, and it could not be reasonably expected that Union soldiers would take any pains to support an institution which has caused so much evil. Southerners are shocked at seeing negro soldiers, while they forget that other civilized nations employ them, and that they have only to cross the Gulf, as the writer has done, to see African soldiers on duty in the streets of Havana, having been received into the service of her Most Catholic Majesty, the Queen of Spain.

XXXI. THE PRESIDENTIAL ELECTION.—In this state of affairs. any suitable pretext was sufficient to precipitate the country into a revolution, more especially, as there was no effort on the part of the government to guard against it. The election of Mr Lincoln, the candidate of the Republican party, afforded the opportunity to Southern fire-eaters, so long and ardently desired, of dissolving all political connection with the North. and immediate secession was the remedy, which. they maintained, would render the South great and prosperous. They confounded the Republican party with the abolitionists, and as the latter had previously been so insignificant in strength as only to excite their contempt, they were driven to the last degree of desperation, to think that a President should be elected, substantially, by their support; and so it was represented to the people. Those who knew better, held up the Republicans as being the most odious of human beings, and not a poll was opened, nor even a vote cast in the South for Mr. Lincoln. In fact, there was so little regard for liberty of thought or action, that one would have been stoned for voting the Republican ticket. Although it was well known to journalists that the most radical Republican had no thought of interfering with slavery in the old States, but simply wished to prevent its spread in the new Territories, still they represented to the Southern people that the object was not only to free all their slaves, but also to subjugate and oppress the whole South. The Democrats, too, had so long ruled with undisputed sway, that they might have embraced a much slighter opportunity than that presented by the negro question, to dispute the right of the new party to rule. Other presidential elections had been boisterous and fraught with danger, but this had known no precedent. The consequence was, that reason could not be heard, and passion, based on false prejudices and erroneous premises, together with a full determination to separate from the North, ruled the day, and the South soon found herself in hostile array against the government, without regarding the national glory, and without sitting down first and consulting whether she was "able with ten thousand to meet him that cometh with twenty thousand."

XXXII. FORT SUMTER.—Soon after the Southern chiefs had succeeded in arousing the

masses to the highest pitch of war feeling, they
began to organize armies and present a threaten-
ing front towards the national government, which
found itself totally unprepared, through accident,
imbecility, or design, to arrest their progress, or
even to receive, in a suitable manner, the honored
chief magistrate of the nation, at its capital.
Although the people in the loyal States were by
no means so impulsive and passionate as those
of the South, and may be supposed to have felt
very much like a sportsman who rises from the
table with his pockets well filled; yet, there was a
calm and determined air, based on the consciousness of having legitimately elected the President,
which made them inwardly resolve to support him,
regardless of consequences. Although the President was scarcely heard of from the time of his
election till he took his seat, and many prominent
men in the South represented to the people that
secession was a mere form, and that there would
be no war, yet it was hard for any true American
to realize the fact; and those politicians who
proclaimed peaceful separation, and induced,
perhaps, the majority to follow them on that
ground, have incurred a dreadful responsibility,
if they knew better; and if they did not, they

were unworthy, as ignorant pretenders, of the confidence of the people. Fort Sumter, in Charleston harbor, was garrisoned by a small number of United States troops, and the insurgents made their first violent outbreak by bombarding and capturing the fort and garrison, and the pitiable sight of the stars and stripes being trailed in the dust by Americans, was first witnessed, and the blow was felt by every loyal heart, though the sentiment in the South was stifled. Forbearance could last no longer, and the indignation of the people of the loyal States burst forth in all its fury.

XXXIII. Seizure of Government Property.—As soon as it became publicly known in the South that secession was inevitable, the leading politicians, who were then in power, but likely to lose their influence in the national government, on account of the defeat of their party, took advantage of the favorable opportunity afforded by the excitement of the populace, to occupy, with the assistance of the voluntoor military companies, all the forts, arsenals, and other property within their limits, belonging to the general government. This was the more easily effected, as the United States had, at that time, scarcely the shadow of an army, and seemed to rely on the honesty of mankind, or the sacredness of its institutions, as a sufficient protection against domestic traitors, as well as foreign enemies. Even the few national troops stationed at Southern points were so depressed or discouraged by the magnitude of the defection, that they surrendered on the first summons; while many officers, sorrowful to tell, from their Southern origin, or from the effects of the general contagion, were led to espouse the rebel cause, and lift their impious hands against the government which had educated them to defend it. The Janizaries, though foreign mercenaries, were never so faithless to the Turk. Thus, the Southern States found themselves at once in peaceable possession of their whole territory, with abundant materials of war, which had been wonderfully increased by government officials favorable to their cause, while the authority of the United States disappeared as if by the influence of a magic wand. In fact, the change seemed to be so wonderful, and so effectual, that it was difficult to realize the fact, and the hearts of thousands bled as they made up their minds to accommodate themselves to circumstances, and to accept separation as a matter in which they had no choice. Many of these same men, for the love of consistency, after they had once resolved, were more unyielding than the original rebels.

XXXIV THE STATE ELECTIONS ON SECESSION.—At the time the question was pretended to be put to the people in the Southern States, whether they would secede or not, they were, to all intents and purposes, as much out of the Union as it was possible to take them, and elections, on such a question, were mere useless formalities, which might be calculated to varnish and gloss over the former action of ejecting the United States authorities, but could not deceive any one who was really alive to passing events. In most of the States conventions were called to pass ordinances of secession, one of which, at least, was not submitted back to the people; while the State of Tennessee was voted out by an ordinary legislature. But what farces were those elections! From the intense excitement to which the masses had been worked up by the inflammable politicians, and the newspapers, it was impossible to stem the torrent, which might have subsided, so as to prevent mischief, had there been a little time for cool reflection; the large conservative *Union* element was pressed downwards and smothered, when at any other time it most assuredly would have triumphed. But the disappointed and defeated politicians knew that the time for their revenge was at hand, and they were determined to seize upon the opportunity. This shows how easily the populace may be gulled, and how communities, under the influence of passion, may act rashly as well as individuals. The Republican party had succeeded, it was true, but the Democrats held a majority in Congress, and Judge Douglas asked in a speech, "what harm could the President do?" Besides, it was plain that the South, by a violent course, would lose the support of a party of friends at the North, and, at the same time, jeopardize her own happiness by a great and unequal contest; while, if she had acted entirely on the defensive, her cause would have been doubly strong. Popular sentiment on the secession and slavery questions ran so high that the supporters of the Union were compelled to work indirectly; or, to speak more truly, belonging to the more conservative and modest portion of the

people, they were indiscreet enough to form a
Cöoperation party, by which it was contended
that all the Southern States should act together,
which course they knew would take time, and,
perhaps, defeat the secessionists. Some Union
men were not willing to vote at all, as they could
not conscientiously embrace either of the parties,
since they both avowedly contemplated the
destruction of the Union. But even as it was,
it is thought that the secession voters in several
of the States were in the minority How different would have been the result, had the elections
taken place at a time when the people could have
been guided by reason, instead of coming, as they
did, in the wake of the great Republican presidential election, when they were blind with
prejudice and passion, and incapable of taking
deliberate action !

XXXV OTHER QUESTIONS.—Many subjects
of vital importance are discussed in private conversation by men who, from their modesty, are
considered ordinary individuals; and more bril
liant thoughts and useful ideas are spoken than
are ever written. The most abstruse sciences
spring from ordinary subjects, which are fully

understood when treated in a plain manner, and yet, most books of learned writers are so full of unusual terms and technical names, that they are totally without interest, or not easily comprehended. Much mystery is also thought necessary in matters of government, and Senators and Ministers are accustomed to monopolize this species of knowledge, especially in unlimited democracies, where they continually proclaim to the people what tenets must be adopted and maintained, always provided they themselves are supported. The truth, however, is, that all the important elements of politics are exceedingly simple, and may be easily understood by ordinary observation, as they grow out of the acts and necessities of every day life. These thoughts may be considered presumptuous and common place, and some of the suggestions here made will doubtless be looked upon as new, and unsupported by authority; while others, again, will appear familiar, as topics long worn out, and therefore devoid of interest. It is true, nothing new may be said, but the object is to apply what is old to the present time. When a poet writes a work, it is because he has something to say, and he says it. When a novelist writes a romance,

he wishes to make a name, teach some moral les-
son, or, what is less meritorious, simply to amuse,
without any ulterior object. The style adopted
in this writing is the most common and uncov-
ered, and what is said is not clothed by fancy,
fiction, or ornament, but plain subjects are treated
in a plain manner If the established order is
perfect, it will stand the test of examination, but
if some of its parts are found to rest on weak foun-
dations, these should be repaired and strengthened. But in this country, where thousands
of journalists have been continually publish-
ing their plans, theories, and doctrines, for so
many years, in the boldest and most confident
manner, without improving the government,
the same right cannot be denied to others,
though their efforts may prove equally unavail-
ing. These subjects are here briefly treated,
partly for amusement, and partly for exercise,
with the humble hope, also, that they may prove
useful matters of reflection, as they relate entirely
to the practical concerns of the country At all
events, the endeavor to account for the causes of
the fatal events which have befallen the nation,
and prevent their recurrence in the future, should
occupy the minds of our wise men; and if any-

9

thing exceptionable is found here, it may be rejected without injury and something better adopted. Many of the old subjects of dispute, which, but a few short years ago, were held up as vital to the interests of the people, are now no longer spoken of, except occasionally by those who speak of the causes of the war. Now, it is clear, that negro slavery was the immediate cause of the war, as a President palpably opposed to that institution was elected, and the slave States thereupon seceded. But the laxity of public morals, the excited and partizan character of politics, together with the immoderate and ultra extremes to which democratic principles were carried, were, beyond question, the grand, primary and disorganizing elements which came near destroying the government. Still, many obstinate men, who are unwilling to be convinced, pretend, with a serious air, that there were other reasons, far more weighty, why the American people were unable to live united.

XXXVI. THE TARIFF —Those who pretend that slavery had no hand in bringing on the war, are apt to allege that the great tariff laid upon foreign manufactures, for the purpose of compelling the Southern people to purchase Northern goods, is calculated to render the South tributary to the North, and consequently, that such a burden is incompatible with the freedom and equality of the Southern States. This subject has been long before the people of the United States, and probably every one will be ready to assert that he fully understands it; but what is said here, is not advanced as being infallible, or as arising from any great experience or study ; and, doubtless, to do the subject full justice, great financial ability and practice would be necessary   To a man of ordinary observation, however, it is clear that the government must be supported either by direct taxation or by its export and import duties.   The fine theories of Fenelon, in his model government, holding that ports should be thrown open, and the commerce of all nations allowed to pass freely, have not much sanction among the practical nations of the world. People, as a general rule, abhor the payment of direct taxes more than any other connec-tion existing between them and the sovereign power, and if they are obliged to contribute largely in that way, it will be difficult to make them understand that the government is good, however much public affairs may otherwise prosper. But if the government is supported principally by the duties laid on commerce, the consumer still pays it, though he does not perceive it, and he is more satisfied with his burden, besides, this method weighs heavier on articles of luxury, which might be dispensed with, and is, at the same time, more favorable to the poor. Still, there are some nations which carry this principle so far as almost to exclude foreign commerce from their ports, and whenever that takes place, the genius and enterprise of a people are too much restricted. Returning, then, to the question of the South being compelled to pay higher for goods manufactured at the North, on account of the tariff on foreign goods, which excludes them from the Southern market: it is true, also, that there is a tariff on foreign sugars, by which the Southern product is protected. Besides, there are other Southern products which are, or might be, protected in the same way, as an offset to the protection afforded to Northern manufactures, and if Massachusetts makes shoes, and Louisiana makes sugar, they may mutually aid and protect each other   But why should such nice distinctions and points of objection be raised? If all the States contribute towards the support of the general government, some more, and some less, yet they all participate in the benefits to be derived from the protection arising from their united power, and no petty differences should ever be allowed to dim the luster of the bright constellation of this Western hemisphere.

XXXVII. NATIONAL BANK.—One great, leading idea of Henry Clay, the National Bank, is about to be established by the war. The Treasury of the United States being independent, and its specie being deposited in its own vaults, so long as the public administrators remain faithful to their trust, the credit of the government can never go down. There is nothing that binds people together so much as their interests. Had there been a National Bank, or a large issue of Treasury Notes, there never would have been any war. Every man interested in the stock of the bank, or having in his possession notes of the government, would have opposed secession. As it was, the banking and exclusive systems of the different States had a tendency to fly off from the central power, and it was not difficult to persuade every man that not only he had no interest in the national government, but that the same was a useless burden and expense, which it would be well to get rid of. It is said that the principal strength of England consists in her national debt, and doubtless the Bank of England is one of the strongest bulwarks of her nationality But, aside from the political aspect of the question, a national paper currency adds greatly to the commerce of a widely extended commercial people. The great issues of bills and bonds by the government incline some to the opinion that they will never be redeemed, and that they will share the fate of the Continental money ; but it must be remembered that the resources of the government are unlimited, and that after the rebellion is put down the nation will come forth like the phœnix, more perfect and beautiful than ever.

XXXVIII. CONQUEST.—In the new order of things established in such parts of the South as have been occupied by the Union armies, it is quite common to find in the public prints such words as, "conquest," "conquerors," " conquered," and others equally unmeaning and silly How can a nation conquer itself, unless, indeed, the reduction of insurgents, who never had any real or legitimate possession of the country, or any part of it, and who ought to be put upon the footing of foreign invaders, can be converted into such a meaning? But this use of offensive terms by letter writers and editors who have never conquered any thing, shows sectional and anti-national vanity, which can do no honor to any particular part of the country, and is calculated to wound the sensibilities of those who have always been equally loyal with themselves. Thousands of men at the South, notwithstanding intimidation by Confederates and devastation by Federals, have always been Union men at heart; not that they love the South "less," but the nation "more." Although individual enemies may be conquered, and their property captured and confiscated, still, the territory of South Carolina, as well as that of New York, belongs to the American people. The bearing towards the South should be rather that of compassion, than insult; and, to the honor of the bravest soldiers be it spoken, those in actual service in the field have been, usually, the most liberal and indulgent. It is the placemen, the fancy officers and cotton speculators that are most to be feared, as they linger behind the armies, in cities, and hang on the rear, insulting equally loyal and disloyal people, preying, like harpies, upon their substance. Every one must admit that it is proper that the goods of traitors should be confiscated to the government, and brave soldiers have always been allowed some license to plunder. But neither the government, nor those who fight, are much benefited by the present captures of war; and as all are Americans, both conquerors and conquered, (to use such terms,) more caution should be used than is observed in the sacking of the cities of one nation by another. However, it cannot be expected that large armies will handle the sections they pass through with gloves on, or that a war of such magnitude could be carried on without great annoyance and injustice to private interests, and also to personal comforts; but the war cannot last always, and it is to be hoped, that with the return of the palmy days of peace all these troubles will pass away

XXXIX. VACANCY OF STATE GOVERNMENTS. Much difficulty is raised by some, respecting the anomalous condition of the Southern States as they are re-occupied by the armies of the government, and the despicable usurpers of the power of the people are driven ignominiously before them. It is pretended that the State governments have become obliterated, and that it is necessary to form new States, which must be regularly re-admitted into the Union. The advocates of this doctrine have chiefly in view the abolition of slavery, and consider that as paramount to the re-establishment of the government, hoping that no State would be allowed to re-enter without first freeing her slaves. It is also convenient for placemen and adventurers to disfranchise the South and thereby hold the country as conquered provinces, so that they can maintain their importance, and make their fortunes. Still, it is proper for the government to continue its military occupation until such time as the local and municipal governments may be entrusted to the people with safety The government should not relinquish its possession until the State is fully recovered; and an election for Governor, or for the purpose of forming a new Constitution, in one corner, would not only be unfair towards loyal citizens in those parts not recovered, but it would be a mere farce. In regard to slavery, it

10

has received such a blow by this war, which has been commenced by the South herself, that it can never recover, and if the Southern people are allowed to free the negroes in their own good time, they will like it much better than if it is done to their hand, and it will be better for the country   But why are the State governments no longer in existence?   May not the law exist, though it cannot be enforced?   The acts of rebellion and secession, being all illegal, were void, and could not affect any thing legally existing previously.   Nothing enacted then should be adopted now, except from necessity and for the public good.   So soon as the usurpers are driven away, the laws and the constitutions of the different States remain as valid as ever, and although the offices are vacant, all that is necessary is to elect new officers under the constitutions and laws. A State, however, may at any time form a new Constitution, provided it is legally done under the authority of the United States.   If a mob should seize upon the corporation of the city of New York and murder all the incumbents of office, and continue to occupy the place for the space of one week, under certain rules and regulations of their own, can it be pretended, that after the mob had been dispersed by the government forces, and the city restored to the people, the charter would be forfeited, or the city laws become extinct? The same is the case with the rebellion, only it is on a larger scale: all its acts are illegal, and change nothing. Any other view would amount to a recognition of the Southern Confederacy

XL. THE FOUNDERS OF THE GOVERNMENT WERE DECEIVED.*—When the wheels of the government of the United States were first set in motion, it was confidently hoped by the great and good men of the age, that a temple of liberty had been reared which should be as enduring as the most perfect work of man. It was considered that the utmost degree of perfection had been reached in the science of government, and that nothing had been neglected which could contribute to the happiness and prosperity of the American people. The exact species of republican government, formed by American statesmen, had not hitherto been adopted, although, in ancient times, there were illustrious examples of Republics formed on more crude and simple

*NOTE.—The four succeeding sections were suggested by an esteemed friend during an evening's conversation.

principles. In regard to the theory of the government, nothing could be more beautiful, and it was eminently well suited to the virtuous people of that age, who had been sorely tried by the war of independence, and felt a patriotic love of country. But governments should not be made for a day, nor for an age, but for time. And yet, these statesmen, notwithstanding their want of experience in the new system, formed a much more conservative government than the present, which has been so changed in the different States, by popular sovereignty, and the elective system, as to lower the standard of public affairs. Scarcely had three-fourths of a century passed when the nation was convulsed from center to circumference by an unprecedented and devastating war, which never would have occurred had the government been so perfect as it was represented, for it should have been so constituted as to foresee, guard against, and prevent such a catastrophe, which was likely to destroy, at least for a time, the very principles upon which the republic had been formed: liberty and the rights of property. In fact, early in the progress of the civil war it was necessary to declare martial law in many places, suspend the *habeas corpus*, and do many other things imcompatible with universal freedom. So it is evident, that the government framed by Washington and his coadjutors is defective, or, at least, not adapted to the present generation ; and it is also evident, that a government should be so constructed as to suit all coming ages.

XLI. THERE HAS BEEN NO PROGRESS, BUT THE PEOPLE HAVE RETROGRADED.—It is commonly asserted, that we live in a very advanced age of civilization, and that vast improvements have been made since the last generation. The contrary is true. The American people have gone back and degenerated much faster, during the same space of time, than the Roman people did in the decline and fall of the Empire. In the time of the Revolution, and long afterwards, the people acted from principle and patriotism. They were a strong, manly and generous race, and were accustomed to esteem honor and reward merit. They could afford to live on moderate means, and considered honest poverty no disgrace. Tho hardy pioneer, who was willing to forego the comforts of civilized life, and felt happy in the enjoyment of the ample liberty afforded by his

country, was honored and esteemed in age, and
held up to the rising generation as an example
worthy of imitation. The intimidation of voters
at the polls would have been punished as a
high crime. How changed are the people now!
Wealth is the standard of respectability, and the
whole tendency of. the American people has
become excessively venal. Education, merit,
principle, knowledge, are considered matters of
secondary importance, and ignorance, well bol-
stered with money, exacts and receives unqualified homage. Who has not seen the wealthy
bankrupt received in society, when he should
have been frowned upon by every honest man?
While on the other hand, the poor but honest
debtor received no encouragement, when he had
parted with his last dollar to pay his just cred-
itors. But success is the motto now, and so
wealth is acquired the means are little regarded.
What wonder, then, that governors and State
officers, in such a general wreck of moral worth,
were the first to forget their oaths of allegiance,
and treacherously seize upon the property and
funds of the United States? That virtue and
love of country which existed in the beginning,
have been lost, and however much the people may

have increased in riches, railroads and telegraphs, if they lack that principle, honor, and moral worth possessed by their ancestors, they have degenerated and not improved.

XLII. THE FOUNDATIONS OF GOVERNMENT.

All governments, whatever their forms may be, possess the same essential principles; and, however numerous their species, they all rest on the same foundation, to-wit: the executive, the legislative, and the judicial departments. The government of the United States has all these parts admirably arranged, and, theoretically, there can be no better government; but it is the people who are not suited to the government. It is a government suited to a virtuous and vigilant people, but not to a careless, mercenary people, who forget their country, and almost their God. In the early ages of the world, governments were more unsystematic and despotic. Often, all the powers of government were centred in one man, and men were taught to obey and respect superiors, while the idea of democratic liberty obtained but little favor. It is natural for men to follow leaders, and the greater the opportunities presented in governments for designing men to lead them astray, the greater will be the danger of the overthrow of the government, and the establishment of anarchy or absolute empire. A politician appears, who is condemned at first, by all, as extravagant, and still, when the popular fury is up, he is chosen for a leader, and the state is overturned. Such was the case in the rebellion. such are the people. A striking example of this is seen in the history of Jefferson Davis, who, in the beginning, was considered throughout the South, (except in his own State, where, by the force of oratory. he had gained the ascendancy over great numbers,) to be a hair-brained fanatic and "fire-eater;" but so soon as the temperature of the populace was afterwards raised to that of his own inflammable composition, this same man was selected as the champion of the South, to maintain the very principles which had formerly been condemned.

In modern times the powers of government have been better distributed, and, perhaps, in none more nicely balanced than in the United States. But may not this fine theory of government be the opposite extreme of despotisms, where all power is united in one man? Both fable and science teach that the middle course is the best. One thing is certain, the nature of man is always essentially the same, and the same fundamental principles must be employed for his government. Laws must be made, rulers must execute and enforce them. And it is impossible for any people to prosper who base not their government on the eternal principles of right.

XLIII. THE INFALLIBILITY OF THE GOVERNMENT.—The American people have been accustomed to consider the United States government as perfect in every respect, without even admitting the possibility of any radical defect in its structure, which might be improved by the new lights arising from experience. Hence, there has been a sort of reluctance to change any essential feature of the government, for fear of relapsing into the monarchical form, or for fear of destroying the fabric which had been so universally received as unexceptionable. The people have been diffident of their own powers, and relied entirely on the work of their forefathers as being founded in wisdom. And although they were fearful of any important and necessary reform, they have gradually allowed themselves, under the influence of demagogues, to innovate

11

on the conservative systems first established, until the original features are now scarcely discernible, and the unbridled license of ultra democratic principles has brought public authority into contempt, and left society unprotected and exposed to unrestrained violence. The changes heretofore made have not been in the right direction, and have injured both the General and the State governments instead of improving them. But why should the people of to-day hesitate to change any important principle of the government if it is found, by experience, to be defective, when their ancestors had courage enough, while it was but an experiment, to found a whole system? The discovery of faults is the true road to improvement. The present generation must rely on themselves, and cannot depend entirely upon the dead. Although the founders of the Republic of the United States were wise and virtuous men, whose memories are entitled to great respect, still, they were men, liable to err, and could not foresee and provide for the wants of a future age. If people were always the same, the matter would be different; but history shows that a virtuous race rarely occurs, and its duration is generally short· hence, governments

should be so constructed as to provide for degenerate as well as prosperous days.

XLIV STATE RIGHTS.—The grandest heresy
of the age has been the doctrine that each State
was a separate and independent sovereignty, and
upon this principle the rebellion was nurtured,
and the founders of the apochryphal Confederacy
went so far as to concede to every State the right
of withdrawing at pleasure. What a wonderful
nation that would be! A nation where all its
component parts would crumble at every freak,
and be liable to decomposition at any moment!
Such a course, in the beginning, was necessary to
the success of their cause, but it is idle to suppose
that they would respect such an absurdity, when
their power was once firmly established. No
State has a right to levy war, make treaties with
foreign nations, establish mails, or do any other act
which is exclusively exercised by independent
sovereigns. Then, what rights have the separate States? They have the right to make local
and domestic laws, relating to their own jurisdic-
tion, but they have no right to do any thing which
may contravene the sovereign power of the
United States. The army and navy, and even

the militia, are under the control of the United States, so that the separate States have no power, except in a civil way, and there can be no independent sovereignty without force to uphold it. They form parts of that government, and possess limited powers for home government, just as a corporate city may act within its charter, but it can do nothing which has for its object the destruction of the power which created it. The people chartered both the States and the nation, and the States were established first; but it was competent for them, the source of power, to say to the States, when they established the government of the United States, "you are subordinate creatures, and we now appoint this new power, which shall be superior to you, for which purpose we invest it with all the extraordinary faculties of an independent nation." But, on the theory that independent sovereignty belongs to the separate States, the existence of the government of the United States becomes a myth, as its independent sovereignty would be incompatible with theirs. It might be aptly remarked, in such a case, "nor can one England brook a double reign of Harry Hotspur and Prince of Wales." But, aside from all law, or ingenious arguments, as to the independent sovereignty of the States, and whether it is legally and constitutionally so or not, the question naturally arises, whether or not it is better to have thirty-six or seven petty nations, independent of each other and all the world besides, or one broad. glorious national Republic, which will fill the heart of every true American with pride, and emulate the greatness of the Roman Empire?

XLV THE CONSTITUTION.—In many instances, the enemies of the country have tried to use the Constitution as a weapon against the re-establishment or perpetuity of the government of the United States. The Executive in office, prior to the war, was afraid to take any steps to put down the insurgents and preserve the Union, lest that sacred instrument should be violated. During the progress of the war, it has been the constant habit of the opposition to cry out against severe measures, rendered necessary by the times, and to try to influence the people against the administration, which was charged with the arduous and responsible duty of bringing back to their allegiance six or eight millions of rebellious people. These representations have been to the effect, that the administration committed violations of the Constitution, wilfully and perversely, when really it is the interest of those in power to act for the best, not only on account of the public welfare, but for their own reputation, therefore, the animosity of the opposing party must arise principally from their desire to obtain, through popular influence, the possession of the administration themselves, and possibly, in some cases, from their innate hostility to the government. But what is the Constitution ' It is the fundamental law of the nation. It is not the nation. The nation may exist without it, as many nations do exist without formal or written constitutions. A part of the Constitution is the oath of the President, by which he undertakes to preserve, perpetuate and defend the nation. Everything which is necessary to that end should be done by him. If a case should arise where it would be necessary to go counter to the Constitution to save the nation, he should not hesitate to do it, because it would be his sworn duty; and it would be stupid to say that the government should be lost merely on account of some defective clause in the organic law   Not but that the Constitution is as perfect, in most respects, as it is possible for any instrument to be, but still, it is necessary to look more to the substance than to the form. There can be no doubt of the existence of the United States as a nation, since she has been recognized as such by all nations, and she has exercised the most sovereign prerogatives of power from her first establishment to the present day So the greatness of the American people is not a dream, and if such a thing could be possible, that the Constitution should be blotted from existence, the nation would still exist. The *Constitution* means also the moral being of the nation itself, as well as the instrument on which the organic law is written. They must not be confounded, and although the instrument is of the greatest importance as the basis and charter of liberty, yet the nation is of still greater importance, as it gives a greater guaranty to that safeguard of human happiness. To illustrate the distinction here made, it will be necessary to use the analagous principles contained in the following well known passage of law "A contract must not be confounded with the instrument in writing by which it is witnessed. The contract may subsist, although the written act may, for some defect, be declared void; and the written act may be good and authentic, although the contract it witnesses be illegal." The foundation of the government of the United States is more reasonable and perfect than the commencement of almost any other nation, since it was formed deliberately by the people, who properly provided for their rights and liberties, whereas, most other nations have been established by usurpation and conquest, and the liberties of the people have been the slow growth of centuries, having been considered encroachments on the royal prerogatives.

XLVI. INDEPENDENCE.—This word has a peculiar charm for the American people, and perhaps no other is more often a' used. The independence of one nation from the control or support of another, is certainly a desirable thing, and no nation is entitled to the name which is unable to maintain this position; for otherwise, it would be a mere dependency The term independence, however, is used in America as almost synonymous with liberty, as both were obtained about the same time. National independence is also distinct from individual independence, which is more limited in its nature, and subjected to more definite and immediate restrictions; but in order to maintain national independence, it is necessary that the component parts should be subservient to, and dependent on, the nation itself. Then, again, in a larger sense, no nation is entirely independent, though it acknowledges no superior, since it should yield to the eternal principles of justice; and unless it does so, misfortune and adversity generally overtake it. So that really, there is no independence, and no liberty of an unrestricted character. Whenever the one or the other, in public or in private, is carried so far as to overstep the limits of right, there is some law to check and chastise the offender. Certain States have ignored the supreme law of the land, and made war on an unoffending government. The consequence is, that a whole people suffer, and enjoy little or no liberty in any part of the country But the cry of independence, raised by artful politicians, is sufficient to cause the people to rush to arms without consideration or reason. The people of the South would be independent of the government of the United States only to lose their own independence and liberties, which they place in the hands of demagogues, who afterwards become tyrants. In this

12

case, however, there never was so little cause of complaint, as the government of the United States was the most lenient towards its citizens of any other in the world, and no act of tyranny was committed. There might be some meaning in the words, independence and liberty, if used by a people deprived of representation, and oppressed by the tyrannical acts of an absolute despot, but when used by Americans as the watch-words of revolution and freedom, it shows that they employ them without comprehending their signification, or that they were unable to bear the prosperity afforded by peace and plenty, and began to fight for what they already possessed. But to carry the principle of independence to its greatest extent, not only every State should be independent, but every city, hamlet and individual citizen would have the right to set at defiance the laws and ordinances enacted for the common good. Liberty and independence, like all things else, must be understood and enjoyed in a moderate degree, otherwise their abuse becomes destructive to the well being of society, and their sacred names become powerful instruments for evil.

XLVII. THE PEOPLE.—All power is derived
from the consent of the governed, is the doctrine
upon which political leaders like to expatiate.
This is true, and so simple that it would seem
almost useless to state the proposition, unless in
opposition to the ancient theological creed that
monarchs reigned by divine right. It is clear
that the people, in a practical point of view, are
the source of State power, for without people in
the beginning, no superstructure could be reared,
and there would be no need of the incorporeal
and moral being called the nation. But experience has shown that the people always find it
necessary to establish a government, and that
they cannot govern themselves *en masse*, notwithstanding the flattery of electioneering politicians,
that every American citizen is a sovereign, and
that he is superior to the government. In the
former sense, it is true that he is superior, as he
is one of the people, and the people are the
source of power; but it is folly to say that the
people govern after the government is established:
and there is a difference between the two, for
otherwise it would be useless to have any government at all. The people being the source of
power, it behooves them to so construct their

government that it may rule in the most enlightened and liberal manner, and, at the same time, be able not only to maintain its existence, but also to protect them in the enjoyment of their rights and liberties. It is not proper, by praising up the people, and descanting on the greatness of democratic institutions, for personal popularity perhaps, to bring the government and its officers into contempt, as every one is interested in the dignity and respect due to them. The people are too near the President. The government is not sufficiently elevated to insure it either dignity or respect.

But, by making the word people a sort of demi-god, politicians have been enabled to turn each other out of office, and, for the sake of place, to create undue prejudices against incumbents, and at the same time use the government itself as a mere plaything. The consequence is, that the people do not rule, but they are used and abused by political leaders, whose chief efforts are directed towards the promotion of party or private interests, without regard to the national welfare. There is a well known principle, that whenever great and extraordinary changes, inequalities and fluctuations occur, without sufficient natural causes, there is danger to the subject which experiences them. The American people have been, for many years, so peculiarly subject to great excitement, and a desire to feed upon some new and wonderful rarity, that it can only be accounted for from the endless political agitations which had, to some extent, educated them to that sort of life. But it would be to the interest of the people if they could bring about such a state of things as would emancipate themselves and the government from the rule of demagogues and election bullies, and at the same time place the government upon a higher footing, which would entitle it to respect, and preserve the country in a more quiet and dignified condition. This would protect it from the sad effects of reckless and popular excitement such as that which brought about the present war. It is necessary to plead the cause of the people against the people.

XLVIII. STRONG GOVERNMENT.—The present war has developed the necessity of maintaining an army Formerly, it was common to say that the United States, being a government of the people, who governed themselves, it was useless

to undergo the expense of subsisting a standing
army, as it would be impossible for the people to
become discontented with their own government,
and make war upon themselves, and that in the
event of a foreign war, the volunteer system
would produce soldiers enough. But some of
the people have become dissatisfied and made
war on the government, by which the whole
people are in danger of losing the government
as well as their liberties. The military power
was so weak and so little encouraged, that it not
only failed to make the nation respected, but it
was looked upon with contempt at home and
abroad, and the principal leaders in the South
were enabled to commit treason, openly and
without restraint, there being no power to check
or awe them in their perjured and treacherous
career. Many of the officers of the regular
army, who had been educated and supported by
the government, were so little animated by the
esprit de corps, owing to the insignificant strength
of the military power of the United States, that
they were ready to resign on the first outbreak,
and allow themselves to be influenced by popular excitement or sectional prejudices, losing
sight of the great moral fact that they were the

nation's pledge for its safety   Had there been an army of fifty thousand men in the South on the first act of treason being committed, and a Jackson at the helm of the government, it requires no assurance to state, that the war would not have happened: and what an inconsiderable sum would have been adequate to the support of such a number of military men, when compared with the untold millions expended in this war! The great moral effect of a military force to maintain the national rights would have strengthened the hearts of patriots and struck terror to the faithless governors and government officers, who had sworn to defend the United States, but boldly and openly proclaimed their intention of destroying it, thereby holding themselves up as examples to be followed by the people, and luring them on to ruin and destruction. So it would appear that the people need some force to protect themselves from their own excitement, as well as from the artful machinations of ambitious and unfaithful officials. Finally, it is necessary that a nation should be sufficiently warlike, and have an adequate force to maintain itself against foreign and domestic enemies, to preserve order and enforce the laws, as well as to command the respect of mankind.

Government is necessary to mankind, and many dangers beset their rights and liberties, "therefore, let any prince or state think soberly of his forces."

XLIX. The Election of the President will always Cause War.—As hath been said heretofore, the great public commotions caused by the excitement attending the election of President have often produced serious alarm to the well wishers of the nation, and the immediate precursor of the civil war was the election of a Republican President in the year 1860. But war is almost the inevitable consequence of these general elections, which involve the whole people, from one side of the country to the other, in one simultaneous struggle for power. The great partizan character of the issues at stake, is calculated to stir up animosities and create false and groundless prejudices, which mislead the people, and make those enemies who have every reason to be friends. But the grand motive power of the politicians who manage these matters, is self-interest, which usually conflicts with the public welfare. By elevating to the presidential chair one who belongs to his party, the office-seeker may well afford to spend a few months in electioneering with the people, the majority of whom, being engaged in agricultural and commercial pursuits, and having but little time for reflection, are easily aroused and prejudiced by specious arguments, so that by the time the election takes place the undue bias and unreasonable excitement, created by the increased sympathy of the multitude, becomes altogether uncontrollable. The truth cannot be understood, and although there may not be really much difference between the two parties, the opposing factions find it to their interest to magnify mole hills into mountains, in order to draw the crowd, exalt their own merits, and detract from those of their adversaries. It was always said, that the election excitement would do no harm, as it subsided always immediately upon the election of the president; but this proved untrue on the election of A. Lincoln, and before the heated pulse of the nation could be brought down to its usual temperature, the high mettled bloods of the country, taking advantage of the feverish condition of the patient, *precipitated* the South out of the Union. This did not happen in the early establishment of the

13

United States, because the people were virtuous, and had a respectful veneration for the model Republic, which was then fresh from the hands of its architects, and was deemed by all to be a perfect work. In those days, such a thing as rebellion against such a government was hardly conceivable, and to have talked of dismemberment and secession would have been considered sacrilegious. Afterwards, however, when sectional interests sprung up, and the mild rule of the government caused it to be but little respected, it was not uncommon, in the national congress, to listen to the doctrines of States' Rights and Nullification, which were the incipient stages of treason. But now, since this cruel civil war has deepened the roots of sectional prejudices, it would be strange if many Presidents were elected, in the popular and exciting way, without war, except by the aid of an army, and even then it would be dangerous.

L. THE STRONG SIDE WILL ALWAYS ELECT THE PRESIDENT.—It requires no sagacity to foresee that the strongest section will always elect the President whenever the sectional interests of the country are diametrically opposed to each other. In the late election the question was tested and decided. The North and West represented free labor, the South slave labor, and their interests were so antagonistic that they drew such an overwhelming majority to the cause represented by the Northern candidate, as almost to amount to a unit, while in the South, had a vote been cast for that candidate, it would have been held a criminal offence. Thus the two sections were arrayed against each other, and the issue was as distinct as if the two sides had been separate and distinct nations of different races of people. But the section in the North was the strongest; therefore, it elected the President. The two sections being so different from each other in institutions and interests, the excitement attending the election of President was calculated to arouse the active elements of that antagonism, in fact, it was the greatest danger to which the country could have been exposed, under such circumstances, and notwithstanding the hostile institutions of the two sections, with a different Constitution, whereby the strife produced by the election could have been avoided, the nation might have flourished in peace for ages. This instance has happened, and it has proved the proposition. The present war may efface the institution of slavery, which, in all probability, created the sectional difference, and, perchance, the whole country may become equalized in its interests . but who can tell what new questions may arise in the distant future, which will create equally as great difficulties as slavery has done, and bring about equally as great differences in the interests of the opposing sections? You have the Atlantic and Pacific possessions, the East, the West and the South, all different in soil, climate and productions, and at any time some new opposing interest may arise, which will cause the different sections to act as units, as heretofore, and seize upon the fair opportunity afforded by the Presidential election to turn the popular enthusiasm into unrestrained clamors for war. That danger should be provided for But should the South, or any other minor section, continue long to have interests opposed to those of the other sections, the consequence would be, that the President would continually be elected by the strong section, and the weak section would have no voice in his choice, so that injustice would be done, and it would have to be held. in all probability, against its will, which would be directly contrary to equal and free republican principles.

Now, if by calling a convention of the people and adopting some plan in the Constitution by which these great dangers could· be avoided, and at the same time, a fixed and permanent executive established, without deviating too far from the democratic form of government, it would, doubtless, add greatly towards perfecting the work of our ancestors, and prove of vast benefit to posterity, as the means of preventing the calamities of war, and preserving the national power and glory in peace and tranquility

LI. ROTATION—It is much easier to discover errors, or what may be considered such, than it is to avoid them, and it often happens that the remedy or amendment is worse than the original; so that whatever is proposed here may be likewise liable to objection, and is simply offered as the humble conviction of an ordinary citizen, with the hope that some remedy may be found for existing evils. If, however, it has been demonstrated, as is believed, that the election of the President, directly, is dangerous to the liberties of the people, as well as to the perpetuity of the national existence, it is to be hoped that the question may be thoroughly examined, and that the Constitution may be changed, so far as it may be found to be defective. One plan might be adopted whereby the President would be chosen by fate, and the people relieved of all trouble in the matter, while the danger to which hereditary monarchies are exposed, of having sovereigns born naturally imbecile, and unfit to govern, would be avoided. It is the system of rotation. Let the oldest Senator, for instance, be the President for life, and at his death, the next oldest, etc. Here, the advantage of having a fixed executive would be positive. That is the greatest secret of governments—it is what all nations have striven for; and the system of hereditary monarchies has been adopted with no other view. So the end is attained, it is immaterial whether the ruler is designated by God, Fate or the People. Men must have something certain to look to as the head, and without that certainty, all becomes confusion and chaos. Venice and Rome are examples. But, if you can find a system which will be equally as certain as that of birth, and at the same time secure a leader of ability, it will be vastly superior to that of hered-

itary monarchies, which depend altogether on
the freaks of fortune for the talents of their sovereigns. Rotation is equally as certain as the
monarchical system—the latter is determined by
birth, the former by death, besides, the transition,
so to speak, is equally as smooth and uninter-
rupted. No commotion of the people takes place,
and the legitimacy of the executive can never be
doubted. That is of vast force. Let it be known
by the people that this is the one, marked by
destiny, to preside over them, and it will be difficult to seduce them from his standard. There
can be no fraud there; no question. In a contest between two Presidents elected by the people, where one is duly elected and the other a
pretender, the advantage is always on the side of
law, because the masses are just, if not deceived,
how much more would they cling to the
undoubted President, marked by the death of
his predecessor, where deception and mal-prac-
tice would be of no avail! The remedy of this
defect in regard to the executive would be so
great that it would of itself naturally correct
nearly all the minor evils spoken of heretofore.
But, says one, why take away the hope of every
American citizen of being President by the force

of his great and transcendent talent, as he may attain that position if the opportunity is afforded? The answer is simple only one out of thirty millions can be President, and it is not proper to neglect the welfare of the whole for his sake. Besides, the most talented man is seldom chosen. The change from one President to another would be sudden and unlooked for, and the new executive would be installed in his office almost before the people would be aware of the fact, while, with the old plan, the people know the day on which the votes are to be cast for President, and the day on which he is to be inaugurated, so that they prepare themselves long beforehand for political battles, which become general, and convulse the body politic throughout the land, greatly endangering, as has been shown, the quietude of society, as well as the national existence.

It is the common practice of politicians to present only that which is popular, whether it is based on truth or not. You must not propose any change in the mode of choosing the President, because, say they, it would be too radical, (that is, too great a change,) and contrary to received ideas: but, if the present mode is erroneous, there ought to be something more

powerful than custom or belief, to allow error to
continue to prevail over truth.

LII. Nothing Anti-Republican is Proposed.

For fear that the writer might be misunderstood
by his fellow-citizens, or misrepresented by public
flatterers, it may be necessary to state distinctly,
that nothing here said is intended as favoring or
proposing a monarchy or empire, and that whenever such words have been used, it has been for
the purpose of explaining as far as possible the
nature of men and governments. The monarchical or hereditary form of government is opposed,
on the ground that it is not sufficiently rational;
as the government, by the mere chance of birth,
may fall into the hands of a weak prince, during
whose minority, or term of incapacity, bad men,
factions, counsellors or regents may ruin the
nation; for it is necessary, although cabinets
may be much depended on, that the national chief
should have some sense of his own. Nothing
could be more unacceptable than the change of
the name of the Republic of the United States,
and every native American should be devotedly
attached to democratic institutions, since they
have afforded, until lately, liberty and happiness
14

to a great people. No one should desire to change
the name *President*, and the Congress should be
preserved intact. But it is simply the mode of
choosing the President which is under consideration, and the objections to the general election
system are sufficiently patent to demand a remedy Neither is it pretended that the Republican form of government is impracticable, but
simply that it has been carried to extremes, and
that if it were somewhat modified in some of its
features, as found necessary by time and experience, it would be the best government in the
world. It may be said that the President by
rotation would have too much power; that being
so long in the Senate he would create a party;
and that the other branches of the government
would be too much under his control. The plan
may have its objections, as nothing human is
perfect, but it is simply contended that it would
be better than the four years' system. If there
would be danger of the President having too
much power, it might be limited in the beginning and the powers of Congress increased. It
is the common report, and without investigation
may be taken as true, that the President has
more power than the monarch of Great Britain,

and still, the President's term is short, while the other is permanent; but this is a matter which depends on the original grant of power, and as the issue of the President by rotation would have no more chance for the presidency than the son of any other citizen, and the tenure of the office would, in the nature of things, be of short duration, no danger could grow out of the excess of power in the executive. As to his creating a party, the danger from that source could never be half so great as before, when, under the Jeffersonian doctrine, to the victors belonged the spoils, without regard to patriotism or merit. The plan of rotation, however, would be eminently democratic, as well as decorous, for the President would spring from the people, and might be the son of a carpenter, who, by a long course of rectitude and industry, had been elevated and continued in honorable place.

LIII. A Bad President.—It might be alleged that the oldest Senator in Congress would be too much exhausted by age to fulfil the duties of the office, and that by the system of rotation the country might occasionally have a bad President. The same thing often happens under the old system, but the chances of a good President would be better under the system of rotation, than under the other, since the oldest Senator would have to be a man of undoubted ability, of tried integrity, and of all the other virtues which insure a long tenure of office conferred upon one well known by his constituents; while under the elective system men, often little known, are taken up by party and elected to the presidency, when their future course cannot be well judged of by their antecedents, and they are only expected to follow the policy of the excited partizans who have elected them. The right of impeachment would always remain, and the Long Parliament demonstrated that the liberties of the Anglo-Saxon race cannot be trampled under foot, and that even a haughty prince must succumb to that power. But here, no strong section could force a President, by mere numerical power, on an unwilling people of a weaker section, which would be unfair, unjust and anti-republican. The objection, though, that the President by rotation would be too old, should be fully considered. It cannot have much weight, when it is remembered that all the great men of the nation have continued active and vigorous in intellect up to the moment of death. Webster, Crittenden, Clay, are examples, and in the last years of their lives they would have filled the office of President with power and credit. Let any one who has been familiar with the nation's counsellors look back and search whether or not, at any particular period, the oldest Senator, up to the time of his death, could not have made a good President. In many cases the incumbents would only hold their offices three or four years, and, perhaps, never over eight or ten, so that if now and then there should be a case where the President would be somewhat incapacitated by age, the probability is that he would soon give place to a successor in the due course of nature. But the President is not the administration, he is simply the nucleus around which the cabinet are col lected, and they, or most of them, must be men of talent; so that, in all events, the executive branch of the government would be well administered. However, it is the Congress which is the great bulwark of the liberties of the people, and with the privilege of always selecting its members they would, at the same time, elect the President indirectly, though it might be by the smallest State in the Union. The government would still be sufficiently democratic, and the elections of Congressmen could never cause any disruption, as they would be local, and held in different States, at different times; so that while one State might be wrought up to some excitement, its neighbor would be in a quiescent condition, and neutralize its effects. Under this system the President would take his seat with the accumulated dignity of a long and useful life. He would not be exposed to the envy and vituperation of the defeated and opposing factions, while the government would move onward with that good order and decorum consistent with the character of a great nation.

LIV THE PRESENT SYSTEM MIGHT HAVE BEEN WELL SUITED TO FORMER TIMES, BUT IS NOT LIKELY TO PROVE THE BEST FOR FUTURE GENERATIONS.— This great war will doubtless produce some changes in the Constitution, as the statesmen of the country will gain much experience from circumstances which have been produced by the necessities of the times. By remedying the defects of the government as it was, and providing against future dangers, the United States ought to become more perfect and stable than ever before. The system of electing the President by the whole people did very well in the beginning, because there was great morality amongst the people. There was simplicity, industry and patriotism in those times. Such ages do not last long, and a government should be founded to stand also after the people have lost their pristine worth, which generally distinguishes early periods. If in this age, when the Americans have somewhat degenerated on account of their great riches, they cannot hold a general election for President without allowing their passions to plunge them into civil war, for the avowed purpose of destroying the government, how can it be expected that future generations, (which may become still more degenerate,) will be able to escape the dangers arising from presidential elections?

NOTE.—After the author had stated the plan of rotation to Mr. Harper, whom he consulted, he was informed by that gentleman that that was the system of the city government of London, Great Britain, the oldest Alderman being the Lord Mayor, of which fact he was not previously aware.

www.ingramcontent.com/pod-product-compliance
Lightning Source LLC
Chambersburg PA
CBHW030545270326
41927CB00008B/1517